CANA

Travel Guide 2023-2024

Your Ultimate Travel Companion: Exploring Off the Beaten Path - Discovering The Beauty, Wonders, Adventure, And Cultural Insights, Best Places And Must-See Attractions

JOHN S. MARLER

Copyright © John s. marler 2023

Table Of Contents

INTRODUCTION

In the vast tapestry of the world's travel destinations, there exists a land of breathtaking beauty and unparalleled adventure - Canada. In the year 2023, a curious traveler named Sarah found herself on the brink of a remarkable journey, armed with a powerful companion: the Canada Travel Guide for 2023-2024.

Sarah's desire to explore Canada had been burning within her for years, and when she first laid her hands on the guide, she felt an exhilarating rush of anticipation. This guide was no ordinary book; it was a gateway to a world of discovery, a treasure trove of experiences waiting to be unlocked.

Her journey commenced in the bustling city of Vancouver, where the guide's detailed maps and insightful recommendations led her through the diverse neighborhoods, allowing her to savor world-class cuisine and immerse herself in the city's vibrant culture. Beyond the tourist hotspots, the guide unveiled hidden gems like Granville Island, where local artisans weaved their magic into every corner, and where Sarah felt like she'd stumbled upon a secret world of creativity.

With the guidance of the travel guide, Sarah embarked on a remarkable road trip through the majestic Canadian Rockies. The meticulously crafted itineraries ensured she didn't miss a single breathtaking view or hidden gem. She stood in awe before the pristine beauty of Banff National Park, where turquoise lakes mirrored towering peaks. She hiked to the dazzling Moraine Lake, an experience that left her feeling like she'd stepped into a postcard brought to life.

The guide's pages turned, leading Sarah to Quebec City, where the rich tapestry of Canadian history and culture enveloped her. She wandered through the cobblestone streets of Old Quebec, feeling as if she had been transported back in time. The guide even offered helpful language tips and phrases, making her feel like a local as she engaged with friendly Quebecois residents.

Sarah's adventure took her through the Maritime Provinces, where she savored coastline of Nova Scotia, explored th fishing villages of Prince Edward Is...., and indulged in the freshest seafood imaginable. The guide led her to hidden spots known only to locals, ensuring she experienced the true maritime spirit of Canada.

From the enchanting wonderland of Newfoundland and Labrador to the ethereal beauty of the Northern Lights in the Yukon, Sarah's journey was enriched by the Canada Travel Guide 2023-2024. It was her constant companion, offering insider tips, advice on accommodations, and guidance on the best times to visit each destination.

Yet, it wasn't just about the places she visited; it was the people she met along the way. The guide emphasized cultural experiences and local encounters, enabling Sarah to form genuine connections with Canadians from all walks of life. She shared stories around campfires, danced at powwows, and attended music festivals, making her feel like an honorary member of the Canadian family.

As Sarah's incredible journey neared its end, she realized that the Canada Travel Guide 2023-2024 had transformed her adventure into an unforgettable odyssey. It had allowed her to explore not just the well-known tourist spots, but also the heart and soul of Canada. She had delved deep into its vibrant cities, pristine wilderness, and diverse cultures, all while feeling supported and guided every step of the way.

With a heart full of gratitude, Sarah recognized that the Canada Travel Guide 2023-2024 had been her trusted companion, helping her create memories that would last a lifetime. It had transformed a simple trip into an extraordinary voyage of discovery, leaving her with a deep love and appreciation for the beauty and diversity of Canada.

Sarah's journey was a testament to the power of the Canada Travel Guide 2023-2024. It had not only been her guide but also her confidant, opening doors to experiences she could have only dreamed of. It had made her journey through Canada's hidden treasures not just an adventure, but a life-changing exploration of a remarkable nation.

Chapter 1

Welcome to Canada

Canada, the second-largest country in the world by land area, is a land of breathtaking natural beauty, diverse cultures, and warm hospitality. From the rugged peaks of the Canadian Rockies to the bustling streets of Toronto and the historic charm of Quebec City, Canada offers a wealth of experiences for travelers.

Diverse Geography and Regions

One of Canada's most striking features is its diverse geography. From the vast wilderness of the Canadian Shield to the pristine lakes of Ontario, and from the coastal rainforests of British Columbia to the rolling plains of the Prairie provinces, each region offers unique landscapes and adventures. Whether you're an outdoor enthusiast, a cultural explorer, or a city lover, Canada has something for everyone.

Cultural Mosaic

Canada is often described as a cultural mosaic, with people from all corners of the globe calling it home. This diversity is reflected in its rich tapestry of languages, cuisine, and traditions. You'll have the opportunity to experience the fusion of cultures, from French-speaking Quebec to the multicultural neighborhoods of Vancouver and Toronto.

Planning Your Visit

Before you embark on your journey to Canada, it's essential to plan your visit carefully. Consider factors such as the time of year you want to travel, your budget, and the activities you wish to experience. Canada has distinct seasons, each offering its own set of attractions, so make sure to align your trip with your interests.

Travel Tips

To ensure a smooth and enjoyable visit, here are a few travel tips to keep in mind:

1. Travel Documents: Check the visa and entry requirements for your country of origin. Ensure your passport is valid for the duration of your stay.

2. Weather Preparation: Pack appropriate clothing for the weather in your chosen region and season. Canada experiences everything from hot summers to frigid winters.

3. Budgeting: Plan your budget wisely. Canada can be expensive, but there are ways to save, such as using public transportation or cooking your meals.

4. Safety: Canada is generally a safe country, but it's essential to stay informed about local safety guidelines and emergency contacts.

In this Canada travel guide for 2023-2024, we'll delve deeper into each aspect of your journey, helping you discover the best destinations, navigate the country, savor the local cuisine, and embrace the rich culture. So, get ready for an unforgettable adventure in the Great White North, as we guide you through the wonders of Canada. Welcome to this vast and captivating land!

Planning Your Visit

Planning a trip to Canada requires careful consideration of various factors to ensure you make the most of your time in this vast and diverse country. Whether you're an outdoor enthusiast, a culture lover, or an urban explorer, thoughtful planning can help you create an itinerary that suits your interests and budget.

Choosing the Right Time to Visit:

Canada experiences four distinct seasons, each offering its unique charm. Consider your preferred activities and the climate you're comfortable with when deciding when to visit:

1. Spring (March to May): Witness the awakening of nature, blooming flowers, and milder temperatures. It's a great time for outdoor activities and exploring cities without the summer crowds.

2. Summer (June to August): Enjoy warm weather and longer daylight hours, ideal for hiking, water sports, and festivals. Tourist hotspots can be crowded during this peak season.

3. Autumn (September to November): Experience vibrant fall foliage and cooler temperatures. This is an excellent time for scenic drives, hiking, and enjoying the changing colors.

4. Winter (December to February): Embrace the snowy wonderland and partake in winter sports like skiing and snowboarding. Cities transform into festive wonderlands during the holiday season.

Creating an Itinerary:

Canada's vastness means you'll need to narrow down your destinations to make the most of your visit. Here are some considerations:

1. Top Cities: Explore major cities like Toronto, Vancouver, Montreal, Quebec City, and Ottawa, each offering a unique cultural and urban experience.

2. Natural Wonders: If you're a nature enthusiast, prioritize national parks like Banff, Jasper, and Gros Morne, where you can hike, camp, and witness breathtaking landscapes.

3. Cultural Exploration: Immerse yourself in Canadian culture by visiting museums, historic sites, and attending local festivals.

4. Off the Beaten Path: Discover hidden gems and less-visited regions for a more authentic and tranquil experience.

Budgeting for Your Trip:

Canada can be an expensive destination, but there are ways to manage your expenses:

1. Accommodation: Consider a mix of hotels, hostels, and vacation rentals to suit your budget.

2. Transportation: Research transportation options and book flights and intercity travel in advance to secure better deals.

3. Dining: Explore local eateries and street food for affordable dining experiences alongside occasional splurges at fine restaurants.

4. Activities: Prioritize must-do activities and budget accordingly. Look for city passes and discounts on attractions.

Travel Documents and Logistics:

Ensure your trip goes smoothly by taking care of essential logistics:

1. Visa and Entry Requirements: Check the specific visa requirements for your country of residence and apply well in advance.

2. Passport: Ensure your passport is valid for the entire duration of your stay in Canada.

3. Health and Insurance: Consider travel insurance and familiarize yourself with any health precautions or vaccinations required.

4. Currency and Banking: Exchange some currency before your trip or use local ATMs. Inform your bank of your travel plans to avoid card issues.

By carefully planning your visit to Canada, you can create an itinerary that aligns with your interests and ensures a memorable and enjoyable experience in this vast and diverse country.

Essential Travel Tips

Traveling to Canada, or any destination, can be a rewarding experience when you're well-prepared. Here are some essential travel tips to help ensure a smooth and enjoyable journey:

1. Travel Documents: Before you go, check your passport's expiration date and any visa requirements for Canada. Ensure you have all necessary documents in order.

2. Weather Awareness: Canada's climate varies widely by region and season. Pack appropriate clothing and check the weather forecast for your destination.

3. Health Precautions: Consult your healthcare provider for any recommended vaccinations or medications. Travel insurance can also provide peace of mind.

4. Currency Exchange: Familiarize yourself with the local currency, and consider exchanging some money before your trip. Credit cards are widely accepted, but it's wise to carry some cash.

Transportation: Research transportation ⌐ns in advance, especially if you plan to move between cities or explore remote areas. Public transportation and rental cars are common choices.

6. Safety Awareness: Canada is generally a safe destination, but it's still essential to be cautious. Keep an eye on your belongings, avoid walking alone in unfamiliar areas at night, and follow local safety guidelines.

7. Communication: Purchase a local SIM card or international roaming plan for your phone to stay connected. Download useful travel apps, such as maps and translation tools.

8. Language: English and French are the official languages in Canada. Learning a few basic phrases in either language can be helpful, especially in Quebec.

9. Tipping: Tipping is customary in Canada, with 15-20% of the bill being a common practice in restaurants. Be sure to tip taxi drivers and service staff accordingly.

10. Emergency Contacts: Keep a list of important phone numbers, including the local emergency services and your country's embassy or consulate in Canada.

Remember that flexibility and a sense of adventure can enhance your travel experience. Embrace the local culture, try new foods, and engage with the people you meet along the way. With these essential travel tips in mind, you'll be well-prepared to explore the beauty and diversity that Canada has to offer. Safe travels!

Chapter 2

Exploring Canada's Diverse Destinations

Canada, known for its stunning landscapes and vibrant cities, offers a wide array of destinations to explore. From the Atlantic to the Pacific, and from the Arctic to the Great Lakes, each region has its unique charm and attractions. Here are some must-visit destinations in Canada:

1. Toronto, Ontario:
- Canada's largest city and a cultural hub.
- Explore the iconic CN Tower and diverse neighborhoods.
- Enjoy world-class dining, shopping, and entertainment.

2. Vancouver, British Columbia:
- Surrounded by mountains and ocean.
- Ideal for outdoor enthusiasts with hiking, skiing, and water sports.

- Experience a diverse food scene and vibrant arts culture.

3. Montreal, Quebec:

- A blend of French and Canadian culture.
- Explore historic Old Montreal and visit world-class museums.
- Savor exquisite cuisine, including famous bagels and poutine.

4. Quebec City, Quebec:

- A charming and historic city.
- Wander through the cobblestone streets of Old Quebec, a UNESCO World Heritage site.
- Discover French culture and cuisine in a picturesque setting.

5. Banff National Park, Alberta:

- A pristine mountain paradise.
- Hike among turquoise lakes, majestic glaciers, and abundant wildlife.
- Experience the beauty of Lake Louise and Moraine Lake.

6. Jasper National Park, Alberta:

- A serene wilderness in the Canadian Rockies.
- Explore the stunning Icefields Parkway, home to the Columbia Icefield.
- Go stargazing in a designated Dark Sky Preserve.

7. Ottawa, Ontario:

- Canada's capital city.
- Visit Parliament Hill, museums, and historic sites.
- Enjoy festivals and events year-round, including Canada Day celebrations.

8. Niagara Falls, Ontario:

- A natural wonder and popular tourist destination.
- Witness the awe-inspiring falls from various vantage points.
- Explore nearby attractions like the Butterfly Conservatory.

9. Prince Edward Island:

- Known for its red sand beaches and Anne of Green Gables heritage.
- Relax on pristine shores and savor fresh seafood.
- Experience the island's rich cultural history.

10. The Maritimes (Nova Scotia, New Brunswick, and Newfoundland and Labrador):

- Discover maritime culture, rugged coastlines, and charming fishing villages.
- Explore the Cabot Trail, Bay of Fundy, and Gros Morne National Park.
- Enjoy fresh seafood and friendly hospitality.

11. The Yukon and Northwest Territories:

- A remote wilderness for adventurous travelers.
- Witness the Northern Lights and explore vast expanses of untouched nature.
- Experience Indigenous cultures and traditions.

12. British Columbia's Islands (Vancouver Island, Gulf Islands):

- Escape to island life with lush forests and coastal beauty.
- Explore Victoria, Tofino, and the Gulf Islands' picturesque landscapes.
- Enjoy outdoor activities, wildlife viewing, and island culture.

Canada's diversity is its strength, and each destination offers a unique experience. Whether you're seeking natural beauty, cultural immersion, or urban adventures, Canada has something to captivate every traveler. Explore these diverse destinations and discover the true essence of the Great White North.

Top Cities and Regions

Canada boasts a rich tapestry of cities and regions, each offering a unique blend of culture, natural beauty, and distinctive experiences. Here are some

of the top cities and regions to explore in this vast
and diverse country:

1. Toronto, Ontario:

- Canada's largest city, known for its
  cosmopolitan vibe.
- Explore iconic landmarks like the CN Tower
  and Royal Ontario Museum.
- Enjoy a diverse culinary scene and vibrant
  neighborhoods.

2. Vancouver, British Columbia:

- Surrounded by mountains and ocean,
  offering outdoor adventures.
- Hike in nearby national parks, such as
  Grouse Mountain.
- Embrace the city's diverse culture and
  stunning natural scenery.

3. Montreal, Quebec:

- A vibrant city with a European charm.
- Stroll through the historic streets of Old
  Montreal.

- Savor French-inspired cuisine and experience lively festivals.

4. Quebec City, Quebec:

- A charming and historic city with a strong French influence.
- Explore the cobblestone streets of Old Quebec, a UNESCO World Heritage site.
- Enjoy a taste of authentic French culture and cuisine.

5. Ottawa, Ontario:

- Canada's capital city, rich in history and culture.
- Visit Parliament Hill, national museums, and historic landmarks.
- Experience festivals and events, including Canada Day celebrations.

6. Banff National Park, Alberta:

- A stunning mountainous region with pristine landscapes.
- Hike to turquoise lakes, glaciers, and see abundant wildlife.

- Discover the beauty of Lake Louise and Moraine Lake.

7. Jasper National Park, Alberta:

- A tranquil wilderness in the Canadian Rockies.
- Drive along the scenic Icefields Parkway.
- Stargaze in a designated Dark Sky Preserve.

8. Niagara Falls, Ontario:

- A world-famous natural wonder and tourist attraction.
- Witness the breathtaking falls from various viewpoints.
- Explore nearby attractions like the Butterfly Conservatory.

9. Prince Edward Island:

- Known for its charming red sand beaches and Anne of Green Gables heritage.
- Relax on picturesque shores and indulge in fresh seafood.
- Immerse yourself in the island's rich cultural history.

10. The Maritimes (Nova Scotia, New Brunswick, and Newfoundland and Labrador):

- Discover maritime culture, rugged coastlines, and fishing villages.
- Explore the Cabot Trail, Bay of Fundy, and Gros Morne National Park.
- Savor fresh seafood and warm hospitality.

Canada's cities and regions offer an incredible array of experiences, from bustling urban life to serene natural beauty. Whether you're interested in history, outdoor adventures, or cultural immersion, there's something to captivate every traveler in these top cities and regions across Canada.

Hidden Gems

While Canada's popular cities and national parks are well-known, the country also boasts a treasure trove of hidden gems waiting to be discovered by intrepid travelers. These lesser-known destinations offer unique experiences and a chance to escape the crowds. Here are some of Canada's hidden gems:

1. Gaspé Peninsula, Quebec:

- Located at the tip of the Gaspe Peninsula, Parc national de la Gaspésie is a haven for hikers and nature enthusiasts.
- Explore the rugged beauty of the Chic-Choc Mountains and spot caribou and moose in their natural habitat.

2. Churchill, Manitoba:

- Known as the "Polar Bear Capital of the World," Churchill offers incredible opportunities for bear watching.
- Visit in the fall to witness polar bears gathering on the shores of Hudson Bay.

3. Fogo Island, Newfoundland and Labrador:

- An isolated island that feels like a world of its own.
- Stay at the unique Fogo Island Inn and immerse yourself in the island's rich culture, art, and stunning coastal scenery.

4. Nahanni National Park, Northwest Territories:

- A UNESCO World Heritage site with dramatic canyons, waterfalls, and the incredible Virginia Falls.
- Perfect for wilderness enthusiasts seeking remote adventure.

5. Haida Gwaii, British Columbia:

- Also known as the Queen Charlotte Islands, this remote archipelago offers lush rainforests, stunning beaches, and rich Indigenous culture.
- Explore ancient Haida village sites and experience the vibrant local art scene.

6. Grasslands National Park, Saskatchewan:

- A serene prairie landscape where you can stargaze in a Dark Sky Preserve.
- Spot bison, pronghorn, and coyotes in their natural habitat.

7. Tofino, British Columbia:

- While popular, Tofino's quieter side offers hidden beaches and tidal pools for peaceful exploration.
- Take a hot spring soak at nearby Hot Springs Cove.

8. Gwaii Haanas National Park Reserve, British Columbia:

- Accessible by boat or seaplane, this park combines rainforests, coastlines, and Indigenous heritage.
- Discover ancient totem poles at SGang Gwaay, a UNESCO World Heritage site.

9. Riding Mountain National Park, Manitoba:

- A lesser-known gem for wildlife watching and outdoor adventures.
- Explore boreal forests and spot black bears, elk, and wolves.

10. Drumheller, Alberta:

- Uncover the Badlands of Alberta, known for their unique landscapes and dinosaur fossils.
- Visit the Royal Tyrrell Museum to learn about prehistoric life.

These hidden gems across Canada offer a chance to connect with nature, experience local culture, and enjoy solitude in breathtaking settings. Whether you're seeking remote wilderness or off-the-beaten-path charm, Canada's hidden treasures are ready to be explored.

Chapter 3

Travel Essentials

Preparing for a trip to Canada involves more than just booking flights and accommodation. To ensure a smooth and enjoyable journey, it's essential to pack the right travel essentials and have key plans in place. Here's a checklist of travel essentials for your visit to the Great White North:

1. Travel Documents:

- Passport: Ensure it's valid for at least six months beyond your planned return date.
- Visa: Check if you need a visa to enter Canada and apply well in advance if required.
- Electronic Travel Authorization (eTA): Some travelers may need an eTA to fly to Canada.

2. Health Precautions:

- Travel Insurance: Protect yourself with comprehensive travel insurance covering medical emergencies, trip cancellations, and lost luggage.

- Medications: Carry any necessary prescription medications and a copy of your prescriptions.
- First Aid Kit: Include basic supplies like adhesive bandages, pain relievers, and antiseptic wipes.

3. Finances:

- Currency: Familiarize yourself with the Canadian dollar (CAD) and exchange some currency before your trip.
- Credit Cards: Notify your bank of your travel plans to avoid card issues, and carry at least one major credit card.
- Budget: Plan your daily expenses and set aside emergency funds.

4. Travel Essentials:

- Luggage: Choose appropriate luggage, and pack light while considering the weather and activities at your destination.

- Travel Adapter: Canada uses Type A and Type B electrical outlets, so bring the right adapter if needed.
- Travel Pillow and Eye Mask: Enhance your comfort during long journeys.
- Portable Charger: Keep your devices powered on the go.
- Copies of Important Documents: Make photocopies or digital scans of your passport, visa, and travel insurance. Store them separately from the originals.

5. Clothing and Footwear:

- Weather-Appropriate Clothing: Pack layers, waterproof gear, and warm clothing if visiting in colder months.
- Comfortable Walking Shoes: Ensure they are suitable for outdoor activities and city exploration.
- Swimsuit: Don't forget it if you plan to swim or visit hot springs.

6. Communication:

- Mobile Phone: Unlock your phone for international use or purchase a local SIM card or travel plan.
- Travel Apps: Download essential apps like maps, translation tools, and weather updates.

7. Personal Items:

- Toiletries: Pack travel-sized toiletries and a small medical kit.
- Travel Towel: Lightweight and quick-drying towels are handy for various situations.
- Reusable Water Bottle: Stay hydrated while reducing single-use plastic waste.

8. Travel Comfort:

- Neck Pillow: Ideal for comfortable rest during long flights or road trips.
- Earplugs and Eye Mask: Ensure a good night's sleep, especially in noisy environments.
- Travel Blanket: Stay warm on chilly flights or during transit.

9. Safety and Security:

- Money Belt or Hidden Pouch: Keep your valuables secure while exploring.
- Locks: Secure your luggage and hostel lockers with sturdy locks.

10. Travel Itinerary:

- Printed Itinerary: Have a printed copy of your travel plans, including flight details and hotel reservations.
- Emergency Contacts: Carry a list of important phone numbers, including local emergency services and your country's embassy or consulate.

By ensuring you have these travel essentials in order, you'll be well-prepared for your journey to Canada, allowing you to focus on enjoying the experiences and adventures this diverse and welcoming country has to offer.

Visa and Entry Requirements

Traveling to Canada is an exciting adventure, but it's crucial to understand the visa and entry requirements before you go. Here's a simplified overview:

1. Visa Requirements:

- Tourist Visa: Depending on your nationality, you may need a tourist visa (Visitor Visa or Temporary Resident Visa) to enter Canada for tourism purposes. Check the official website of the Government of Canada or your nearest Canadian embassy or consulate to see if you require a visa.

2. eTA (Electronic Travel Authorization):

- Some travelers, including those from visa-exempt countries, need to apply for an Electronic Travel Authorization (eTA) before flying to Canada. This is an online application and is typically approved quickly, but it's essential to apply in advance.

3. Passport Validity:

- Ensure that your passport is valid for at least six months beyond your planned return date from Canada.

4. Entry Port of Arrival:

- When you arrive in Canada, ensure that you land at a designated port of entry, such as an international airport or border crossing.

5. Immigration and Customs:

- Be prepared to answer questions from Canadian immigration officials about the purpose of your visit, your travel plans, and financial resources. Customs may inspect your luggage for restricted or prohibited items.

6. Proof of Funds:

- It's a good idea to carry proof of sufficient funds to support yourself during your stay in Canada. This can be in the form of bank statements, traveler's cheques, or a credit card.

7. Return Ticket:

- Immigration officers may ask for proof of a return ticket or onward travel plans, demonstrating your intent to leave Canada before your visa or eTA expires.

8. Health and Insurance:

- Canada may require travelers to show proof of health insurance coverage during their stay. Travel insurance is highly recommended to cover medical emergencies.

9. Criminal Record:

- If you have a criminal record, including DUI convictions, you may be denied entry into Canada. It's essential to check with Canadian immigration authorities before traveling.

Remember that entry requirements can vary based on your nationality and the purpose of your visit. It's crucial to check the most up-to-date information and comply with all entry requirements before embarking on your journey to Canada. Failure to meet these requirements could result in denied entry or delays, potentially affecting your travel plans.

Best Times to Visit

Canada's diverse climate means that the best time to visit varies depending on your preferences and the regions you plan to explore. Here's a simplified guide to help you choose the ideal time for your Canadian adventure:

1. Summer (June to August):

- Ideal for: Outdoor enthusiasts, city explorers, and festival-goers.
- Highlights: Pleasant weather, longer daylight hours, and numerous outdoor activities.
- Popular Destinations: Toronto, Vancouver, Banff National Park, and Quebec City.
- Events: Festivals, hiking, water sports, and wildlife viewing.

2. Fall (September to November):

- Ideal for: Nature lovers, leaf peepers, and those who prefer fewer crowds.
- Highlights: Stunning fall foliage, cooler temperatures, and fewer tourists.
- Popular Destinations: Niagara Falls, Prince Edward Island, and the Canadian Rockies.
- Events: Leaf-peeping, wine tasting, and fall festivals.

3. Winter (December to February):

- Ideal for: Snow enthusiasts, skiers, and those who love winter wonderlands.
- Highlights: Snow-covered landscapes, winter sports, and festive holiday markets.
- Popular Destinations: Whistler, Quebec City's Winter Carnival, and Jasper National Park.
- Events: Skiing, snowboarding, ice skating, and Northern Lights viewing.

4. Spring (March to May):

- Ideal for: Early-season hikers, nature admirers, and those seeking milder weather.

- Highlights: Blooming flowers, thawing lakes, and fewer crowds.
- Popular Destinations: Ottawa (Tulip Festival), Vancouver Island, and Montreal.
- Events: Cherry blossoms, hiking, and spring festivals.

Keep in mind that Canada is a vast country, and the climate can vary greatly from one region to another. Research the specific destinations you plan to visit to ensure the best experience during your chosen season. Regardless of when you visit, Canada offers a wide range of activities and experiences to suit every traveler's interests.

Budgeting Tips

Traveling to Canada can be an unforgettable experience, but it's essential to manage your finances wisely to make the most of your trip without breaking the bank. Here are some budgeting tips to help you plan your Canadian adventure effectively:

1. Plan Ahead:

- Create a detailed travel budget that includes transportation, accommodation, food, activities, and miscellaneous expenses.
- Research prices in advance to have a realistic idea of what to expect in Canada.

2. Consider the Season:

- Traveling during the shoulder seasons (spring and fall) often means lower prices for accommodations and fewer crowds, making it an excellent time for budget-conscious travelers.

3. Accommodation Choices:

- Look for budget-friendly accommodation options such as hostels, guesthouses, and vacation rentals.
- Consider staying in less touristy areas to find more affordable lodging.

4. Dining Wisely:

- Save on food costs by exploring local eateries, food trucks, and markets where you can enjoy affordable and delicious meals.

- Plan picnics or pack snacks for days of sightseeing to avoid dining out for every meal.

5. Transportation Savings:

- Opt for public transportation within cities, which is often more cost-effective than renting a car.
- Consider using rideshare apps and carpooling services for shorter trips.
- Take advantage of discount passes or multi-ride tickets for attractions and transportation.

6. Free and Low-Cost Activities:

- Research free or low-cost attractions and activities in each destination, such as hiking trails, city parks, and museums with discounted admission on certain days.

7. Travel Insurance:

- While it may seem like an added expense, travel insurance can save you money in case of emergencies, such as medical issues or trip cancellations.

8. Currency Exchange:

- Be mindful of exchange rates and fees when converting your currency. Compare rates at banks, exchange offices, and ATMs to get the best deal.

9. Budget Tracking:

- Use budgeting apps or spreadsheets to track your expenses during your trip. This helps you stay on top of your spending and make adjustments as needed.

10. Avoid Over-touristed Areas:

- While famous attractions are a must-see, consider exploring less touristy neighborhoods and regions to find more budget-friendly experiences.

11. Special Deals and Discounts:

- Check for discounts and deals on admission tickets, dining, and activities in advance or through local coupon books and websites.

12. Emergency Funds:

- Set aside an emergency fund for unexpected expenses like medical emergencies, lost items, or changes in travel plans.

Remember that budgeting doesn't mean sacrificing the quality of your experience. With careful planning and some cost-saving strategies, you can explore the beauty and culture of Canada without overspending. By adhering to a budget, you'll have peace of mind and the freedom to enjoy all that this incredible country has to offer.

Chapter 4

Getting Around

Canada is a vast and diverse country with a well-developed transportation infrastructure that offers various ways to get around. Here's an overview of the transportation options and tips to navigate Canada effectively:

1. Domestic Flights:
- For long-distance travel between major cities and regions, domestic flights are often the fastest option.
- Consider booking tickets in advance to secure better deals, especially during peak travel seasons.

2. Intercity Buses:
- Intercity bus services connect cities and towns, offering a cost-effective way to travel.
- Companies like Greyhound and Megabus provide extensive routes and schedules.

3. Trains:

- Via Rail operates passenger train services connecting major cities, providing a scenic and comfortable way to travel.
- Consider purchasing rail passes for multi-city journeys to save money.

4. Rental Cars:

- Renting a car is an excellent choice for exploring rural and remote areas, including national parks.
- Make sure to understand Canadian driving laws and regulations, and book your rental car in advance.

5. Public Transportation:

- Cities like Toronto, Vancouver, Montreal, and Ottawa have efficient public transit systems, including buses, subways, and trams.
- Purchase reloadable transit cards or passes for convenience and savings.

6. Ride-Sharing Apps:

- Ride-sharing services like Uber and Lyft are available in many Canadian cities, offering a convenient and often cost-effective way to get around.

7. Ferries:

- In coastal regions and islands, ferries are essential for transportation.
- Check schedules and make reservations for popular ferry routes during peak travel times.

8. Cycling and Walking:

- Many Canadian cities are bike-friendly, with dedicated lanes and bike-sharing programs.
- Walking is an excellent way to explore urban areas and enjoy the scenery.

9. Taxis and Ride-Hailing:

- Taxis are readily available in cities, but they can be more expensive than ride-sharing options.
- Ride-hailing apps like Uber and Lyft provide a convenient alternative.

10. Travel Passes and Discounts:

- Consider purchasing regional or city-specific travel passes for unlimited access to public transportation or attractions.
- Student, senior, and youth discounts are often available for transportation and attractions.

11. Plan Ahead:

- Research transportation options, schedules, and fares in advance to make informed decisions.
- Use travel apps and maps to navigate unfamiliar cities and regions.

12. Safety and Etiquette:

- Follow safety guidelines and etiquette when using public transportation, including offering seats to those in need and obeying local rules.

13. Eco-Friendly Options:

- Canada is increasingly promoting eco-friendly transportation, such as electric buses and bike-sharing programs. Consider using these options to reduce your environmental footprint.

Whether you're exploring the vibrant cities, majestic national parks, or remote wilderness areas of Canada, understanding the transportation options and planning ahead will help you make the most of your Canadian adventure. Enjoy the journey as you discover the beauty and diversity of this incredible country.

Transportation Options

Canada's vast and diverse landscape calls for a variety of transportation options to explore its many wonders. From bustling cities to remote wilderness areas, here's an overview of the transportation choices available to travelers in Canada:

1. Domestic Flights:
- Ideal for: Long-distance travel between major cities and regions.

- Highlights: Speedy and efficient, ideal for covering vast distances.
- Tips: Book flights in advance to secure better deals and check for airlines offering domestic routes.

2. Intercity Buses:

- Ideal for: Budget-conscious travelers exploring cities and towns.
- Highlights: Extensive routes connecting various destinations, cost-effective.
- Tips: Consider bus passes for multiple journeys and be prepared for longer travel times compared to flights.

3. Trains:

- Ideal for: Travelers seeking a scenic and comfortable journey between major cities.
- Highlights: Relaxing and picturesque, a unique way to see the country.
- Tips: Purchase rail passes for flexibility and explore sleeper car options for overnight trips.

4. Rental Cars:

- Ideal for: Exploring rural areas, national parks, and remote regions.
- Highlights: Freedom to set your own itinerary and access less touristy destinations.
- Tips: Understand Canadian driving laws, book in advance, and consider renting an eco-friendly vehicle.

5. Public Transportation:

- Ideal for: Getting around within cities like Toronto, Vancouver, and Montreal.
- Highlights: Convenient and cost-effective, with buses, subways, trams, and commuter trains.
- Tips: Purchase transit cards or passes for savings and familiarize yourself with local transit maps.

6. Ride-Sharing Apps:

- Ideal for: Short-distance city travel in areas served by ride-sharing services.

- Highlights: Convenience and accessibility, often cheaper than taxis.
- Tips: Download apps like Uber or Lyft and check local regulations for ride-sharing services.

7. Ferries:

- Ideal for: Coastal and island travel in regions like British Columbia and Newfoundland.
- Highlights: Picturesque and necessary for accessing certain areas.
- Tips: Check schedules and book in advance for popular ferry routes, especially during peak seasons.

8. Cycling and Walking:

- Ideal for: Exploring bike-friendly cities and enjoying urban areas on foot.
- Highlights: Eco-friendly and leisurely ways to see the sights.
- Tips: Use bike-sharing programs, and remember to follow traffic rules and pedestrian etiquette.

9. Taxis and Ride-Hailing:

- Ideal for: Convenient point-to-point travel within cities.
- Highlights: Easy to find, available in most urban areas.
- Tips: Negotiate fares in advance for taxis, and use ride-hailing apps for price transparency.

10. Eco-Friendly Options:

- Ideal for: Environmentally conscious travelers.
- Highlights: Electric buses, hybrid taxis, and bike-sharing programs in many cities.
- Tips: Opt for these options to reduce your carbon footprint while traveling.

Choosing the right transportation mode depends on your itinerary, budget, and preferences. Whether you're exploring Canada's urban centers, natural wonders, or a combination of both, these transportation options will help you make the most of your Canadian journey.

Driving Tips

If you plan to explore Canada by car, it's important to be aware of the country's unique driving conditions and regulations to ensure a safe and enjoyable journey. Here are some essential driving tips for navigating the Canadian roads:

1. Driver's License and Rental Car:

- Ensure you have a valid driver's license from your home country. International Driving Permits (IDPs) may be required in some provinces.
- If renting a car, confirm that you meet the rental company's age requirements and provide all necessary documentation.

2. Right-Hand Driving:

- In Canada, drive on the right-hand side of the road, with the driver's seat on the left side of the vehicle.

3. Speed Limits:

- Speed limits are posted in kilometers per hour (km/h). Pay close attention to speed limit signs, which may change frequently.

4. Seat Belts:

- Seat belt use is mandatory for all occupants in the vehicle. Failure to wear seat belts can result in fines.

5. Child Safety Seats:

- Children under a certain age and weight must use approved child safety seats or booster seats. Regulations vary by province.

6. Mobile Phones:

- Using a handheld mobile phone while driving is illegal in most provinces. Use a hands-free device if necessary.

7. Alcohol and Drug Use:

- Canada has strict laws against driving under the influence of alcohol or drugs. The legal blood alcohol limit is 0.08%, but it's best to avoid alcohol entirely if you plan to drive.

8. Road Signs and Signals:

- Familiarize yourself with Canadian road signs and signals, which may differ from those in your home country.
- Pay attention to electronic signs that provide real-time traffic and weather information.

9. Wildlife Caution:

- In rural and wilderness areas, be alert for wildlife, especially at dawn and dusk. Watch for road signs indicating animal crossing zones.

10. Winter Driving:

- If traveling during the winter months, equip your vehicle with winter tires and carry snow chains in case of heavy snowfall.
- Be prepared for icy roads, reduced visibility, and potentially treacherous driving conditions.

11. Road Conditions:

- Check road conditions and weather forecasts before setting out on a long drive, especially in remote or mountainous areas.

12. Fuel Stops:

- Plan your route to include fuel stops, as distances between gas stations can be substantial in some regions.

13. Emergency Kit:

- Carry an emergency kit in your vehicle, including items like a flashlight, first aid supplies, blankets, and non-perishable food and water.

14. Rest Stops:

- Take regular breaks to rest and stretch during long drives. Canada has well-maintained rest areas along major highways.

15. Maps and Navigation:

- Use GPS or navigation apps to help you find your way. Offline maps can be useful in remote areas with limited cell phone coverage.

16. Wildlife Caution:

- In rural and wilderness areas, be alert for wildlife, especially at dawn and dusk. Watch for road signs indicating animal crossing zones.

Remember that road conditions and driving regulations can vary by province, so it's essential to research the specific areas you plan to visit. With these driving tips in mind, you can navigate Canada's roads safely and enjoy the stunning landscapes and diverse destinations this country has to offer.

Chapter 5

Accommodation Options

Canada offers a wide range of accommodation options to suit every traveler's budget and preferences. Whether you're seeking luxury, comfort, or affordability, you'll find suitable places to stay across the country. Here's an overview of accommodation options in Canada:

1. Hotels:

- Ideal for: Travelers seeking comfort, amenities, and a range of services.
- Highlights: Hotels in Canada vary from boutique to large chains, offering everything from basic accommodations to luxury suites.
- Tips: Book in advance, especially during peak travel seasons, and consider loyalty programs for potential discounts.

2. Motels:

- Ideal for: Budget-conscious travelers and road trippers.

- Highlights: Motels often offer straightforward and convenient lodging, with parking available right outside your room.
- Tips: Motels are prevalent along highways and in smaller towns, making them a popular choice for travelers exploring by car.

3. Bed and Breakfasts (B&Bs):

- Ideal for: Those seeking a personalized and charming lodging experience.
- Highlights: B&Bs provide cozy accommodations with home-cooked breakfasts and a chance to interact with local hosts.
- Tips: Research and book B&Bs in advance, as they often have limited rooms and high demand.

4. Vacation Rentals:

- Ideal for: Families and groups looking for a home-like atmosphere.

- Highlights: Vacation rentals include apartments, cabins, cottages, and entire homes, offering space, privacy, and self-catering facilities.
- Tips: Use reputable platforms like Airbnb or Vrbo to find and book vacation rentals.

5. Hostels:

- Ideal for: Budget travelers, solo backpackers, and those seeking a social atmosphere.
- Highlights: Hostels provide dormitory-style or private room accommodations at affordable rates. Common areas encourage interaction among guests.
- Tips: Check guest reviews and ratings to choose hostels that match your preferences.

6. Camping:

- Ideal for: Outdoor enthusiasts and nature lovers.
- Highlights: Canada's national and provincial parks offer campgrounds where you can

pitch tents or park RVs amid stunning natural landscapes.

- Tips: Reserve campsites well in advance, especially during peak camping season.

7. Cabins and Cottages:

- Ideal for: Those looking for a rustic and secluded getaway.

- Highlights: Cabins and cottages in rural areas or near lakes and forests offer a peaceful retreat and a chance to connect with nature.

- Tips: Book early, as these accommodations can fill up quickly, particularly in popular vacation spots.

8. Indigenous Accommodations:

- Ideal for: Travelers interested in experiencing Indigenous culture and traditions.

- Highlights: Indigenous-owned lodges, teepees, and cultural centers offer unique cultural and educational experiences.

- Tips: Plan your stay in advance and respect Indigenous customs and traditions.

9. Luxury Resorts:

- Ideal for: Travelers seeking opulence, exceptional service, and world-class amenities.
- Highlights: Canada boasts luxury resorts in picturesque settings, offering spa treatments, gourmet dining, and recreational activities.
- Tips: Splurge on a luxurious stay for a special occasion or to unwind in style.

10. Budget Hotels and Inns:

- Ideal for: Travelers looking for a balance between comfort and affordability.
- Highlights: Budget hotels and inns provide clean and comfortable accommodations without the frills of luxury properties.
- Tips: Check for promotions and discounts when booking budget accommodations.

When selecting accommodation in Canada, consider your travel style, budget, and the destinations you plan to visit. Research, book in advance when necessary, and read reviews from fellow travelers to ensure a pleasant and memorable stay in the Great White North.

Hotels, Hostels, and Rentals

When planning your trip to Canada, one of the most important decisions you'll make is where to stay. Canada offers a diverse range of accommodation options to suit various preferences and budgets. Here's a closer look at hotels, hostels, and vacation rentals, so you can choose the perfect place to rest your head during your Canadian adventure:

1. Hotels:

- Ideal For: Travelers seeking comfort, convenience, and a variety of services.

Highlights:

- Diverse Options: Canada has a wide range of hotels, from luxury resorts to budget-friendly options.

- Amenities: Hotels typically offer amenities like restaurants, bars, room service, fitness centers, and concierge services.
- Consistency: Chain hotels often provide standardized experiences, making them a familiar choice for many travelers.
- Privacy: Hotels offer private rooms and housekeeping services.

Tips:

- Book Early: Especially during peak tourist seasons, booking your hotel in advance ensures you secure your preferred accommodation.
- Loyalty Programs: Consider joining hotel loyalty programs for potential discounts and benefits if you frequently stay with a particular chain.

2. Hostels:

- Ideal For: Budget-conscious travelers, backpackers, solo adventurers, and those seeking a social atmosphere.

Highlights:

- Affordability: Hostels offer some of the most budget-friendly lodging options, with both dormitory-style and private room accommodations.

- Social Environment: Common areas like lounges and kitchens encourage interaction among guests, making it easy to meet fellow travelers.

- Community Vibe: Hostels often organize activities and events, fostering a sense of community among guests.

- Local Insights: Hostel staff can provide valuable tips on exploring the local area.

Tips:

- Check Reviews: Read guest reviews and ratings to choose a hostel that aligns with your preferences for cleanliness, atmosphere, and location.

- Private Rooms: If you prefer more privacy, many hostels offer private rooms alongside shared dormitories.

3. Vacation Rentals:

- Ideal For: Families, groups, and travelers looking for a home-like atmosphere with added space and self-catering facilities.

Highlights:

- Versatility: Vacation rentals include apartments, cabins, cottages, and entire homes, accommodating various group sizes and preferences.
- Privacy: Rentals offer more privacy and autonomy compared to hotels and hostels.
- Local Experience: Staying in a vacation rental can provide a more authentic experience of living like a local.
- Self-Catering: Many rentals come with fully equipped kitchens, allowing you to prepare your meals.

Tips:

- Use Reputable Platforms: Book vacation rentals through trusted platforms like Airbnb, Vrbo, or Booking.com, and read property reviews.

- Check Amenities: Confirm that the rental has all the amenities you need, such as Wi-Fi, laundry facilities, and parking.

When choosing between hotels, hostels, and vacation rentals in Canada, consider your travel style, budget, and the nature of your trip. Each type of accommodation offers unique advantages, so whether you're seeking luxury, affordability, social interaction, or a home away from home, you'll find a suitable place to stay in this vast and welcoming country.

Booking Strategies

Planning a trip to Canada involves more than just choosing your destination and packing your bags. To ensure a smooth and enjoyable travel experience, it's essential to develop effective booking strategies. Here are some tips and strategies to help you book your accommodations, flights, activities, and more:

1. Start Early:

- For popular destinations and peak travel seasons, it's wise to start your planning and booking process well in advance. This includes booking flights, accommodations, and tours.

2. Flexible Dates:

- If possible, be flexible with your travel dates. Sometimes shifting your trip by a few days can lead to significant cost savings on flights and accommodations.

3. Use Fare Comparison Websites:

- Utilize flight comparison websites like Google Flights, Skyscanner, or Kayak to compare fares from multiple airlines and find the best deals.

4. Sign Up for Fare Alerts:

- Subscribe to fare alert emails from airlines and travel deal websites. This way, you'll be notified when there are price drops or promotions for your desired routes.

5. Consider Alternate Airports:

- Check if nearby airports offer more affordable flights. Sometimes, flying into a nearby city and taking ground transportation to your final destination can be cost-effective.

6. Loyalty Programs:

- Join airline and hotel loyalty programs to earn rewards and take advantage of member discounts and perks.

7. Accommodation Booking:

- Read reviews and research accommodations thoroughly before booking.
- Consider booking directly through the hotel's website for potential discounts and added benefits.
- Look for last-minute deals on hotel booking websites and apps.

8. Travel Insurance:

- Don't overlook the importance of travel insurance. Purchase comprehensive coverage that includes medical emergencies, trip cancellations, and lost luggage to protect your investment.

9. Package Deals:

- Explore package deals that bundle flights, accommodations, and activities. These can often provide significant savings.

10. Group Discounts:

- If you're traveling with a group, inquire about group discounts for accommodations, tours, and activities.

11. Visa and Entry Requirements:

- Research visa requirements and apply well in advance to avoid last-minute complications.
- Ensure your passport is valid for at least six months beyond your intended return date.

12. Local Tours and Activities:

- Research and book local tours, activities, and attractions in advance to secure your spot, especially for popular tours.
- Check for combination deals that offer discounts when booking multiple activities.

13. Currency Exchange:

- Monitor exchange rates and consider exchanging currency before your trip for better rates.

14. Research Local Holidays and Events:

- Be aware of local holidays and events that may affect your travel plans. Some attractions may be closed or crowded during festivals or holidays.

15. Stay Informed:

- Keep an eye on travel advisories and COVID-19 related updates from official government sources and the World Health Organization (WHO).

16. Stay Organized:

- Create a travel itinerary or use a travel planning app to keep track of your bookings, reservations, and important travel documents.

By implementing these booking strategies, you'll not only save time and money but also ensure a stress-free and memorable travel experience in Canada. Planning ahead and staying informed are key to making the most of your journey in this beautiful and diverse country.

Chapter 6

Food and Dining

Canada's food scene is as diverse and vast as its landscapes. From coast to coast, you'll find a rich tapestry of flavors, reflecting the country's multicultural heritage and its commitment to using locally sourced ingredients. Here's a glimpse into the culinary delights you can savor during your visit to Canada:

1. Canadian Cuisine:

- Highlights: Canadian cuisine is known for its fusion of Indigenous, French, British, and other international influences. Poutine (fries smothered in cheese curds and gravy), butter tarts, and tourtière (meat pie) are just a few iconic dishes.

- Seafood: Enjoy fresh seafood in coastal regions, with specialties like Atlantic lobster, Pacific salmon, and East Coast oysters.

- Maple Syrup: Sample Canada's famous maple syrup, often drizzled over pancakes, waffles, or used in various dishes.
- Wild Game: Try game meats like venison, bison, and caribou in restaurants specializing in local and Indigenous cuisine.

2. International Flavors:

- Canada's multicultural cities offer a world of culinary options, from Italian and Chinese to Indian and Middle Eastern cuisine.
- Explore ethnic neighborhoods like Toronto's Chinatown, Montreal's Little Italy, or Vancouver's Punjabi Market for authentic tastes.

3. Craft Beer and Wine:

- Canada's craft beer scene has exploded in recent years, with microbreweries and brewpubs offering a wide variety of locally crafted beers.
- Discover the country's wine regions, including the Okanagan Valley in British Columbia and the Niagara Peninsula in

Ontario, known for producing excellent wines.

4. Farmers' Markets:

- Visit farmers' markets to taste seasonal produce, artisanal cheeses, baked goods, and handcrafted products.
- Try the St. Lawrence Market in Toronto or Granville Island Public Market in Vancouver.

5. Indigenous Cuisine:

- Experience Indigenous cuisine, which emphasizes locally sourced ingredients and traditional cooking methods.
- Sample dishes like bannock (a type of fried bread), wild rice, and game meats at Indigenous-owned restaurants and cultural centers.

6. Street Food:

- Canadian cities offer a vibrant street food scene, with food trucks and stalls serving everything from gourmet burgers to international street eats.

- Don't miss the BeaverTails pastries, a sweet Canadian delicacy.

7. Fine Dining:

- Canada boasts numerous Michelin-starred and award-winning restaurants. Indulge in fine dining experiences showcasing seasonal and regional ingredients.

8. Dietary Preferences:

- Canada is accommodating to various dietary preferences, with many restaurants offering vegetarian, vegan, and gluten-free options.

9. Unique Regional Dishes:

- Each region of Canada has its own unique dishes and specialties. Try the lobster rolls in the Maritimes, Nanaimo bars in British Columbia, and tourtière in Quebec.

10. Food Festivals:

- Check for food festivals and events happening during your visit. Canada hosts events like the Vancouver International Wine Festival and the Poutine Fest in Ottawa.

11. Tipping:

- Tipping is customary in Canada, with a standard gratuity of 15-20% in restaurants.

Canada's culinary landscape is an exciting fusion of traditions and innovations, making it a delightful destination for food enthusiasts. Whether you're enjoying street food in Vancouver, savoring French cuisine in Montreal, or indulging in Indigenous flavors in Saskatchewan, Canada's diverse dining options promise a memorable gastronomic journey.

Must-Try Canadian Cuisine

When visiting Canada, don't miss the opportunity to indulge in some of its iconic and delicious dishes. Here are a few must-try Canadian culinary delights:

1. Poutine:

- A Canadian classic, poutine consists of crispy French fries topped with cheese curds and smothered in savory gravy. It's the ultimate comfort food.

2. Butter Tarts:

- These sweet and gooey tarts feature a flaky pastry shell filled with a rich, buttery, and sugary filling. They're a Canadian dessert staple.

3. Maple Syrup:

- Canada is renowned for its high-quality maple syrup. Drizzle this liquid gold over pancakes, waffles, or even ice cream for a taste of Canadian sweetness.

4. Nanaimo Bars:

- Named after the city of Nanaimo in British Columbia, these no-bake bars consist of three delicious layers: a crumbly base, a creamy custard-flavored middle, and a glossy chocolate top.

5. Tourtière:

- A savory meat pie that varies by region, tourtière is typically made with minced pork or a mix of meats. It's a popular dish during the holiday season.

6. BeaverTails:

- These indulgent pastries are stretched and fried to resemble a beaver's tail (hence the name). They're often topped with various sweet toppings like cinnamon sugar or chocolate.

7. Bannock:

- A traditional Indigenous bread, bannock is often fried and served as a snack or side dish. It's incredibly versatile and can be sweet or savory.

8. Smoked Salmon:

- In the coastal regions of Canada, particularly British Columbia, you'll find some of the world's best smoked salmon. Enjoy it on a bagel with cream cheese or as a topping for salads.

9. Peameal Bacon Sandwich:

- A Toronto specialty, this sandwich features peameal bacon (back bacon) coated in cornmeal and fried to perfection, served on a bun with toppings like lettuce and tomato.

10. Bison or Elk Burgers:

- For a taste of the wild, try a burger made from lean bison or elk meat. These game meats offer a unique and delicious flavor.

These Canadian culinary treasures showcase the country's diverse heritage and love for hearty, flavorful dishes. Whether you're exploring the vibrant food scene of a major city or enjoying regional specialties in smaller towns, these must-try Canadian foods will satisfy your taste buds and leave you craving more.

Dining Etiquette

When dining in Canada, following some basic etiquette guidelines can enhance your dining experience and ensure you feel comfortable in various settings. Here's a simple overview of dining etiquette in Canada:

1. Tipping:

- Tipping is customary in Canada. In restaurants, it's standard to leave a gratuity of 15-20% of the bill, based on the quality of service.

2. Reservations:

- Make reservations, especially for fine dining restaurants, to secure your table and avoid long wait times.

3. Dress Code:

- Dress appropriately for the restaurant's atmosphere. Casual attire is acceptable in many places, but upscale restaurants may have a dress code.

4. Arrival Time:

- Arrive on time for your reservation. Being punctual is considered polite.

5. Table Manners:

- Wait until everyone is served before starting to eat.
- Keep your napkin on your lap during the meal, and use it to wipe your mouth.
- Chew with your mouth closed and avoid slurping.

6. Dietary Preferences:

- Inform your server of any dietary restrictions or allergies when ordering to ensure your meal accommodates your needs.

7. Wait for the Host:

- If you're a guest, wait for the host to begin the meal or say "Bon appétit" before you start eating.

8. Mobile Phones:

- Silence your mobile phone and avoid using it during the meal to maintain a distraction-free atmosphere.

9. Conversations:

- Engage in polite and pleasant conversation with your dining companions, but avoid sensitive topics like politics or religion.

10. Paying the Bill:

- When dining with others, it's customary for the person who extended the invitation to pay the bill. If dining with friends, you may choose to split the bill.

11. Tipping at Cafés and Fast Food:

- At casual eateries like cafés and fast-food restaurants, tipping is less common. However, it's appreciated if you received exceptional service.

12. Takeout and Leftovers:

- If you have leftovers, it's acceptable to request a takeout container to bring them home.

13. Alcohol Consumption:

- Canada has legal drinking age limits, which vary by province. Ensure you meet the legal age requirements if you plan to order alcoholic beverages.

14. Expressing Gratitude:

- Saying "please" and "thank you" is common practice in Canada and appreciated in all dining situations.

By adhering to these basic dining etiquette tips, you'll not only enjoy a more pleasant dining experience but also show respect for Canadian customs and hospitality. Whether you're dining in a fancy restaurant or a cozy local eatery, good manners and consideration go a long way.

Chapter 7

Culture and Etiquette

Canada is known for its multicultural society and polite, inclusive culture. Understanding a few key aspects of Canadian culture and etiquette can help you navigate social interactions with ease during your visit:

1. Politeness: Canadians are known for their politeness. Saying "please" and "thank you" is customary and appreciated in everyday interactions.

2. Punctuality: Being on time is important in Canada. Whether you have a meeting or a social engagement, arriving punctually is a sign of respect for others' time.

3. Multiculturalism: Canada is a diverse nation, and Canadians take pride in their multicultural heritage. Respect for different cultures and traditions is highly valued.

4. Greetings: A firm handshake and maintaining eye contact are typical when meeting someone for the first time. Canadians often greet each other with a friendly "Hello" or "Hi."

5. Personal Space: Canadians value personal space. Maintain a respectful distance during conversations and avoid standing too close to others, especially with people you've just met.

6. Queuing: Canadians are patient and orderly when it comes to queuing or waiting in line. Cutting in line is considered rude.

7. Tipping: Tipping is customary in Canada, typically ranging from 15% to 20% in restaurants for good service. Tipping is also common in other service industries.

8. Respect for Nature: Canadians have a strong connection to nature, and there is a general respect for the environment. Littering and harming natural areas are frowned upon.

9. Cultural Sensitivity: Be respectful of cultural differences and sensitivities. Canadians are generally open-minded and accepting, but it's essential to be mindful of diverse perspectives.

10. Language: Canada is bilingual, with English and French as official languages. English is predominant in most provinces, but in Quebec, French is the primary language. Learning a few phrases in the local language can be appreciated.

11. Dress Code: Dress code varies depending on the occasion and region. In major cities, casual attire is common, but some upscale restaurants may have a dress code.

12. Socializing: Canadians are generally friendly and open to socializing. Engage in polite and positive conversations, avoiding controversial topics like politics and religion.

13. Gift Giving: When invited to someone's home, it's customary to bring a small gift, such as wine or chocolates, as a token of appreciation.

14. Cultural Events: Canada hosts a variety of cultural events and festivals. Participating in these events is an excellent way to immerse yourself in the local culture.

15. Respect for Indigenous Peoples: Canada acknowledges and values the contributions of its

Indigenous peoples. Show respect for their cultures, traditions, and history.

By keeping these cultural and etiquette considerations in mind, you can navigate social interactions in Canada smoothly and enjoy a warm and welcoming experience in this diverse and inclusive country.

Social Norms

Understanding social norms is essential when interacting with locals in Canada. Here are some key social norms to keep in mind:

1. **Politeness:** Canadians are known for their politeness and courtesy. Saying "please" and "thank you" is customary in everyday conversations.

2. **Punctuality:** Being on time is important in Canada, whether for business meetings or social gatherings. Arriving a few minutes early is considered respectful.

3. Personal Space: Canadians value personal space and generally maintain a comfortable distance during conversations. Respect others' personal boundaries.

4. Queue Etiquette: Canadians are patient when waiting in line. Cutting in line is considered rude, so wait your turn patiently.

5. Multiculturalism: Canada is a diverse country, and Canadians take pride in their multicultural society. Respect for different cultures and traditions is highly valued.

6. Greetings: A firm handshake and maintaining eye contact are common when meeting someone for the first time. Greet others with a friendly "Hello" or "Hi."

7. Tipping: Tipping is customary, particularly in restaurants. A tip of 15-20% of the bill is standard for good service. Tipping is also common in other service industries.

8. Cultural Sensitivity: Be aware of cultural differences and sensitivities. Canadians are generally open-minded, but it's essential to be respectful of diverse perspectives.

9. Environment: Canadians have a strong connection to nature, and there is a general respect for the environment. Littering and harming natural areas are discouraged.

10. Dress Code: Dress code varies depending on the occasion and region. In major cities, casual attire is common, but upscale venues may have a dress code.

11. Socializing: Canadians are generally friendly and open to socializing. Engage in polite and positive conversations, avoiding sensitive topics like politics and religion.

12. Gift Giving: When invited to someone's home, bringing a small gift, such as wine or chocolates, is a thoughtful gesture of appreciation.

13. Social Equity: Canada values equality and social justice. Discrimination or prejudice based on race, gender, religion, or other factors is strongly discouraged.

14. Indigenous Respect: Canada acknowledges and respects its Indigenous peoples. Show respect for their cultures, traditions, and historical contributions.

By following these social norms, you can build positive relationships and enjoy a respectful and considerate experience when interacting with Canadians in various settings.

Tipping Guidelines

Tipping is a common practice in Canada, and it's an important way to show appreciation for good service. Here are some tipping guidelines to keep in mind during your visit:

1. Restaurants:

- In restaurants, it's customary to leave a tip of 15-20% of the bill before taxes. This percentage can vary based on the level of service you received.

2. Bartenders:

- When ordering drinks at a bar, it's typical to leave a tip of $1-2 per drink or 15-20% of the total bill.

3. Coffee Shops and Cafés:

- Tipping at coffee shops and cafés is optional, but it's common to leave a small tip in the tip jar or for counter service if you received good service.

4. Delivery Services:

- When ordering food for delivery, consider tipping the delivery driver 15-20% of the order total.

5. Taxi and Ride-Sharing:

- For taxi and ride-sharing services, a tip of 10-20% of the fare is appreciated.

6. Hotel Services:

- Housekeeping: Leaving a tip of $2-5 per night for housekeeping services is customary.
- Bellhop/Porter: Tipping $2-5 per bag is standard for assistance with luggage.

- Concierge: Tipping for exceptional service is at your discretion.

7. Tour Guides and Activities:

- Tour guides and activity instructors often rely on tips. Consider giving $5-10 per person for half-day tours and $10-20 per person for full-day tours.

8. Hairdressers and Spa Services:

- For hairdressers and spa services, it's customary to tip 15-20% of the service cost.

9. Tipping Jars:

- Keep an eye out for tipping jars at various establishments, like fast-food counters or food trucks. Leaving small change or rounding up the bill is appreciated.

10. Exceptional Service:

- If you receive exceptional service, don't hesitate to tip more generously. Tipping is a way to reward and recognize excellent service.

11. Bill Calculation:

- Calculate your tip based on the pre-tax total of the bill.

12. Credit Card Payments:

- Most establishments allow you to add a tip when paying by credit card. You can specify the tip amount and total on the receipt.

Tipping is a customary practice in Canada, and it plays an important role in service industry workers' income. By following these tipping guidelines, you can show appreciation for good service and ensure a positive and respectful interaction with service providers during your visit.

Chapter 8

Outdoor Adventures

Canada's breathtaking natural landscapes provide the perfect backdrop for a wide range of thrilling outdoor adventures. Whether you're an adrenaline junkie or a nature enthusiast, you'll find an abundance of activities to immerse yourself in the beauty of the Canadian wilderness. Here are some outdoor adventures to consider during your visit:

1. Hiking:

- Explore Canada's vast network of hiking trails, ranging from easy walks to challenging multi-day treks. Iconic destinations like Banff and Jasper National Parks in Alberta offer stunning trails for all skill levels.

2. Canoeing and Kayaking:

- Paddle through pristine lakes, winding rivers, and coastal waters. Discover the serenity of Algonquin Provincial Park in

Ontario or the rugged coastlines of British Columbia's Gulf Islands.

3. Whitewater Rafting:

- Experience the thrill of navigating turbulent rivers. The Kicking Horse River in British Columbia and the Ottawa River in Ontario are renowned for their whitewater adventures.

4. Wildlife Viewing:

- Canada's diverse ecosystems are home to an array of wildlife. Go wildlife watching for a chance to spot bears, moose, whales, and eagles in their natural habitats.

5. Skiing and Snowboarding:

- In the winter months, Canada becomes a playground for snow sports enthusiasts. Enjoy world-class skiing and snowboarding in destinations like Whistler, Mont Tremblant, and Banff.

6. Ice Climbing:

- Embrace the icy landscapes of Canada by trying ice climbing. Alberta's Johnston

Canyon and Ontario's Thunder Bay offer excellent ice climbing opportunities.

7. Dog Sledding:

- Experience the age-old tradition of dog sledding in regions like Yukon and Quebec. Glide through snow-covered forests and learn about the art of mushing.

8. Mountain Biking:

- Canada's mountainous terrain provides ideal conditions for mountain biking. Explore the renowned trails of British Columbia's North Shore or Quebec's Mont-Sainte-Anne.

9. Zip Lining:

- Soar through the treetops on thrilling zip line adventures. Whistler, British Columbia, and Tremblant, Quebec, offer exhilarating zip line experiences.

10. Rock Climbing:

- Climb to new heights on Canada's challenging rock faces. The Canadian Rockies in Alberta and Squamish in British

Columbia are famous rock climbing destinations.

11. Camping and Backpacking:

- Escape into the wilderness by camping or backpacking. Canada's national and provincial parks provide excellent camping facilities and backcountry experiences.

12. Aurora Borealis Viewing:

- Witness the mesmerizing Northern Lights in northern Canada, particularly in places like Yellowknife, Northwest Territories, and Churchill, Manitoba.

13. Fishing:

- Cast your line in Canada's pristine lakes and rivers. Fishing enthusiasts can reel in a variety of species, including salmon, trout, and walleye.

14. Caving:

- Explore underground wonders in Canada's caves and caverns. The Marble Arch Caves in Newfoundland and Banff National Park's Rat's Nest Cave are popular spots.

Whether you're seeking heart-pounding adventures or serene moments in nature, Canada's outdoor playground offers something for everyone. Make the most of your visit by experiencing the country's natural wonders through these exciting outdoor activities.

Hiking and Nature Exploration

Canada is a paradise for hikers and nature enthusiasts, offering a myriad of opportunities to explore its pristine wilderness. Here's a brief overview of hiking and nature exploration in this stunning country:

1. Hiking Trails:

- Canada boasts a vast network of hiking trails, catering to all levels of experience. From leisurely strolls to challenging backcountry treks, there's a trail for everyone.

- Iconic destinations like Banff, Jasper, and Yoho National Parks in Alberta offer breathtaking hikes amid the Rocky Mountains.

2. Coastal Adventures:

- Canada's extensive coastline provides opportunities for coastal hiking and beachcombing. Explore the rugged shores of Newfoundland and Nova Scotia or the sandy beaches of Prince Edward Island.

3. Wildlife Encounters:

- Canada's diverse ecosystems are home to an array of wildlife. Keep an eye out for bears, moose, whales, and eagles as you venture into the wilderness.

4. National and Provincial Parks:

- Canada's national and provincial parks are treasure troves of natural beauty. Visit places like Pacific Rim National Park Reserve in British Columbia or Gros Morne National Park in Newfoundland for immersive nature experiences.

5. Indigenous Experiences:

- Learn about Indigenous cultures and traditions through guided hikes and nature tours offered by Indigenous communities. Gain a deeper understanding of the land's significance.

6. Birdwatching:

- Canada is a birdwatcher's paradise. Explore birding hotspots like Point Pelee National Park in Ontario or the Bay of Fundy in New Brunswick.

7. Alpine Adventures:

- In the alpine regions, you can embark on high-altitude hikes, witness breathtaking glaciers, and enjoy pristine alpine lakes. Try the Lake O'Hara Alpine Circuit in British Columbia for an unforgettable alpine experience.

8. Forest Retreats:

- Immerse yourself in lush forests and tranquil woodlands. Hike through enchanting old-growth forests in places like Cathedral Grove on Vancouver Island.

9. Mountain Vistas:

- Ascend to mountain peaks for panoramic vistas. The hike to the summit of Mount Royal in Quebec City or Mount Rundle in Banff offers breathtaking views.

10. Wilderness Camping:

- Extend your adventure by camping in Canada's national and provincial parks. Spend nights under starlit skies and awaken to the sounds of nature.

11. Educational Programs:

- Many parks offer guided nature programs, allowing you to learn about the local flora and fauna while exploring the outdoors.

12. Safety and Conservation:

- Prioritize safety by following trail markers, carrying essential supplies, and respecting wildlife. Contribute to conservation efforts by leaving no trace and practicing responsible hiking.

Hiking and nature exploration in Canada offer an unparalleled opportunity to connect with the country's natural wonders. Whether you seek solitude in the wilderness, stunning vistas, or encounters with wildlife, Canada's great outdoors beckon you to explore and appreciate its pristine beauty.

Winter Sports

Canada's long and snowy winters provide the perfect playground for winter sports enthusiasts. From skiing and snowboarding to ice skating and snowshoeing, here's a quick glimpse into the exciting world of winter sports in Canada:

1. Skiing and Snowboarding:

- Canada is renowned for its world-class ski resorts. Destinations like Whistler Blackcomb in British Columbia and Mont Tremblant in Quebec offer pristine slopes and thrilling terrain for skiers and snowboarders of all levels.

2. Ice Hockey:

- Considered Canada's national pastime, ice hockey is more than just a sport; it's a cultural phenomenon. Attend a game or try your hand at a friendly match on a frozen pond.

3. Ice Skating:

- Lace up your skates and glide across outdoor ice rinks, many of which pop up in city centers during the winter months. Iconic rinks like Ottawa's Rideau Canal Skateway offer a unique experience.

4. Cross-Country Skiing:

- Explore serene winter landscapes on cross-country skis. Canada's many trails, including those in Gatineau Park near Ottawa and Lake Louise in Alberta, are perfect for Nordic skiing.

5. Snowshoeing:

- Venture into snow-covered forests on snowshoes, a peaceful and accessible way to enjoy the winter wilderness.

6. Dog Sledding:

- Experience the thrill of dog sledding in regions like Yukon and Quebec. Let a team of enthusiastic huskies lead you through snowy trails.

7. Snowmobiling:

- Snowmobiling allows you to cover vast distances and access remote winter landscapes. Explore designated trails in provinces like Ontario and Newfoundland.

8. Curling:

- Try your hand at curling, a strategic and social sport that's a hit with Canadians. Many communities have curling clubs open to visitors.

9. Ice Fishing:

- Set up an ice fishing shack on a frozen lake and try your luck catching fish through a hole in the ice. It's a quintessential Canadian winter experience.

10. Snowboarding Terrain Parks:

- For snowboarders, terrain parks in ski resorts offer jumps, rails, and halfpipes for freestyle fun. Test your skills in these snow playgrounds.

11. Winter Festivals:

- Attend winter festivals across Canada, where you can watch ice sculptures being carved, enjoy hot beverages by bonfires, and participate in winter-themed activities.

12. Safety First:

- Whether you're skiing down steep slopes or enjoying a leisurely skate, always prioritize safety by wearing appropriate gear and following safety guidelines.

Canada's winter sports scene caters to all levels of experience, from beginners to seasoned athletes. Whether you're seeking adrenaline-pumping adventures or tranquil moments in the snow-covered landscapes, Canada's winter wonderland invites you to embrace the chill and experience the thrills of winter sports.

Chapter 9

Top Attractions And Wonders

Canada offers a treasure trove of attractions that cater to a wide range of interests. From natural wonders to cultural landmarks, here's a glimpse of what you can explore in this vast and diverse country:

1. Niagara Falls:

- Witness the awe-inspiring power of Niagara Falls, one of the world's most famous natural wonders. Take a boat tour to get up close to the thundering falls.

2. Banff National Park:

- Explore the stunning landscapes of Banff National Park in Alberta. Marvel at turquoise lakes, rugged mountains, and abundant wildlife in this pristine wilderness.

3. CN Tower:

- Soar to the top of Toronto's CN Tower for panoramic city views. It's an iconic symbol of Canada's largest city.

4. Old Quebec City:

- Step back in time in the charming streets of Old Quebec City, a UNESCO World Heritage site known for its historic architecture and European ambiance.

5. Parliament Hill:

- Visit Ottawa's Parliament Hill to see the impressive Gothic Revival architecture and experience the Changing of the Guard ceremony during the summer months.

6. Vancouver Island:

- Discover the natural beauty of Vancouver Island, known for its lush rainforests, scenic beaches, and the vibrant city of Victoria.

7. Royal Tyrrell Museum:

- Unearth the mysteries of the past at the Royal Tyrrell Museum in Alberta, home to an extensive collection of dinosaur fossils.

8. Stanley Park:

- Enjoy the green oasis of Vancouver's Stanley Park, where you can stroll, bike, or rollerblade along scenic seawall paths.

9. Peggy's Cove:

- Visit the picturesque Peggy's Cove in Nova Scotia, known for its iconic lighthouse and rugged coastal scenery.

10. Northern Lights:

- Witness the mesmerizing Northern Lights (Aurora Borealis) in northern Canada, particularly in places like Yellowknife, Northwest Territories.

11. The Distillery District:

- Explore Toronto's historic Distillery District, a pedestrian-only zone filled with art galleries, boutiques, and restaurants.

12. Butchart Gardens:

- Immerse yourself in the beauty of Butchart Gardens in British Columbia, a stunning collection of floral displays and landscaped gardens.

13. Capilano Suspension Bridge Park:

- Experience the thrill of walking across the Capilano Suspension Bridge amid the towering trees of North Vancouver.

14. Canada's Wonderland:

- Enjoy family fun at Canada's Wonderland, a popular amusement park in the Greater Toronto Area.

15. Cultural Festivals:

- Attend cultural festivals such as the Calgary Stampede, Montreal Jazz Festival, and Toronto International Film Festival for a taste of Canadian arts and entertainment.

Canada's attractions offer a rich tapestry of experiences, from natural wonders and historic sites to cultural festivals and modern marvels. No matter where you choose to explore, you'll find a wealth of diverse wonders waiting to be discovered in this beautiful country.

Iconic Landmarks

Canada is adorned with a tapestry of iconic landmarks that tell stories of its history, culture, and natural splendor. Here's a glimpse of some of these renowned treasures:

1. CN Tower, Toronto:

- Toronto's CN Tower is an architectural marvel and an iconic symbol of Canada. It offers breathtaking views of the city from its observation decks and revolving restaurant.

2. Parliament Hill, Ottawa:

- Canada's seat of government, Parliament Hill in Ottawa, showcases stunning Gothic Revival architecture and hosts national celebrations, including Canada Day festivities.

3. Quebec City's Old Town:

- The historic streets of Quebec City's Old Town are a UNESCO World Heritage site, where cobblestone streets, centuries-old architecture, and a European ambiance transport you to another era.

4. Banff National Park, Alberta:

- This jewel of the Canadian Rockies boasts turquoise lakes, towering mountains, and pristine wilderness. Lake Louise and Moraine Lake are iconic gems within the park.

5. Stanley Park, Vancouver:

- Stanley Park in Vancouver is a lush urban oasis featuring scenic seawall paths, majestic totem poles, and the stunning Prospect Point lookout.

6. Peggy's Cove Lighthouse, Nova Scotia:

- The Peggy's Cove lighthouse is perched on rugged coastal rocks, making it one of Canada's most photographed and charming landmarks.

7. Royal Tyrrell Museum, Alberta:

- Located in the heart of dinosaur country, this museum houses an extensive collection of dinosaur fossils and offers a glimpse into prehistoric life.

8. Butchart Gardens, British Columbia:

- Butchart Gardens near Victoria is a horticultural masterpiece with vibrant floral displays, themed gardens, and serene walking paths.

9. Hopewell Rocks, New Brunswick:

- These massive flowerpot-shaped rock formations are sculpted by the world's highest tides in the Bay of Fundy.

10. Peggy's Point Lighthouse, Nova Scotia:

- Perched on a rocky shoreline, Peggy's Point Lighthouse is one of Canada's most photographed and picturesque lighthouses.

11. Athabasca Glacier, Alberta:

- Located in the Columbia Icefield, the Athabasca Glacier offers the chance to walk on ancient ice in the heart of the Canadian Rockies.

12. Head-Smashed-In Buffalo Jump, Alberta:

- This UNESCO World Heritage site preserves the history of Indigenous buffalo hunting and features an interpretive center built into the cliffside.

13. Confederation Bridge, Prince Edward Island:

- Connecting PEI to the mainland, this engineering marvel is the world's longest bridge over ice-covered waters and a sight to behold.

14. Magnetic Hill, New Brunswick:

- Experience the optical illusion of rolling uphill at Magnetic Hill, a natural wonder and roadside attraction in Moncton.

15. Haida Gwaii, British Columbia:

- This remote archipelago showcases the rich Indigenous culture and stunning landscapes, including the iconic totem poles of SGang Gwaay.

These iconic landmarks represent the diversity and grandeur of Canada, offering visitors a chance to connect with the country's natural beauty, history, and culture. Each landmark is a touchstone of Canada's heritage and a testament to its enduring allure.

Museums and Galleries

Canada is home to a wealth of museums and galleries that celebrate its rich history, vibrant culture, and artistic creativity. Here's a glimpse into some of the remarkable institutions waiting to be explored:

1. Royal Ontario Museum (ROM), Toronto:

- Canada's largest museum, the ROM, houses a vast collection of art, culture, and natural history artifacts. It's a journey through time and around the world.

2. National Gallery of Canada, Ottawa:

- This iconic gallery showcases Canadian and international art, including the Group of

Seven's masterpieces and an impressive collection of Indigenous art.

3. Canadian Museum for Human Rights, Winnipeg:

- Located in a stunning architectural marvel, this museum explores the struggle for human rights worldwide through interactive exhibits and powerful storytelling.

4. Museum of Anthropology, Vancouver:

- Nestled in the Pacific Northwest, this museum highlights Indigenous art and culture, with a focus on the Indigenous peoples of the Northwest Coast.

5. Art Gallery of Ontario (AGO), Toronto:

- The AGO features an extensive collection of Canadian and European art, including works by the famous Group of Seven and pieces from renowned artists.

6. Canadian Museum of History, Gatineau:

- Explore Canada's rich history through engaging exhibits, including the stunning

Grand Hall featuring Indigenous totem poles and a Pacific Coast indigenous village.

- **7. Vancouver Art Gallery:**This gallery boasts an impressive collection of contemporary and historical art, including works by iconic Canadian artists like Emily Carr.

8. The Rooms, St. John's:

- The Rooms is Newfoundland and Labrador's cultural center, housing art, history, and archives that showcase the province's unique heritage.

9. Royal BC Museum, Victoria:

- Dive into British Columbia's history, natural wonders, and Indigenous culture at this captivating museum.

10. Canadian Museum of Nature, Ottawa:

- Discover the wonders of the natural world, from dinosaurs to gems, in this fascinating museum.

11. Aga Khan Museum, Toronto:

- This museum showcases Islamic art and culture, featuring a stunning collection of artifacts and artworks.

12. Glenbow Museum, Calgary:

- Explore Western Canadian history, art, and culture in this dynamic museum in the heart of Calgary.

13. Museum of Contemporary Art Toronto (MOCA):

- MOCA showcases cutting-edge contemporary art and provides a platform for emerging artists to shine.

14. The Canadian Canoe Museum, Peterborough:

- Learn about Canada's rich canoeing heritage and Indigenous watercraft traditions in this unique museum.

15. Winnipeg Art Gallery:

- Home to one of the world's most extensive collections of Inuit art, this gallery offers a deep dive into Indigenous creativity.

These museums and galleries offer a glimpse into Canada's artistic, cultural, and historical tapestry. Whether you're passionate about art, history, or simply eager to learn, these institutions provide windows to the soul of Canada's diverse heritage and creativity.

Chapter 10

Practical Information

When planning your trip to Canada, it's essential to have practical information at your fingertips to ensure a smooth and enjoyable journey. Here are some key details to help you prepare:

1. Travel Documents:

- Ensure your passport is valid for at least six months beyond your planned departure date. Depending on your nationality, you may need a visa or an Electronic Travel Authorization (eTA) to enter Canada. Check the official Canadian government website for visa requirements.

2. Currency:

- The currency used in Canada is the Canadian Dollar (CAD). Credit and debit cards are widely accepted, and ATMs are readily available. Currency exchange services are also accessible at airports and banks.

3. Language:

- Canada is bilingual, with English and French as official languages. While English is predominant in most provinces, Quebec primarily speaks French.

4. Time Zones:

- Canada spans several time zones, from GMT-3.5 in Newfoundland to GMT-8 in the Pacific Time Zone. Be aware of the time difference when planning your travel.

5. Weather:

- Canada experiences varying climates, so pack accordingly. Winters are cold, especially in northern regions, while summers can be warm and humid. Check the weather forecast for your specific destination.

6. Health and Safety:

- Canada is known for its high standard of healthcare. Travel insurance is advisable to cover unexpected medical expenses. The country is generally safe for travelers, but exercise standard precautions regarding personal safety and your belongings.

7. Electrical Outlets:

- Canada uses Type A and Type B electrical outlets with a voltage of 120V and a frequency of 60Hz. If your devices have a different plug type or voltage, you may need adapters and converters.

8. Transportation:

- Canada offers an extensive transportation network, including buses, trains, and domestic flights. Major cities have well-developed public transit systems. Consider renting a car for exploring more remote areas.

9. Accommodation:

- Canada offers a range of accommodation options, including hotels, hostels, vacation rentals, and campgrounds. Booking in advance is advisable, especially during peak travel seasons.

10. Communication:

- Canada has excellent mobile network coverage. You can purchase local SIM cards for your phone or activate international roaming with your provider. Wi-Fi is commonly available in hotels, cafes, and public spaces.

11. Tipping:

- Tipping is customary in Canada. In restaurants, a gratuity of 15-20% of the bill before taxes is standard for good service. Tipping is also common in other service industries.

12. Taxes:

- Canada has a Goods and Services Tax (GST) and a Provincial Sales Tax (PST) or Harmonized Sales Tax (HST), which vary by province. These taxes are added to the price of most goods and services.

13. Emergency Services:

- The emergency phone number in Canada is 911 for police, fire, and medical emergencies. Canada has a well-organized emergency response system.

By keeping these practical details in mind, you'll be better prepared for your journey to Canada and can focus on enjoying the incredible experiences and beautiful landscapes this country has to offer.

Safety and Health Tips

Ensuring your safety and well-being during your visit to Canada is paramount. Here are some essential safety and health tips to help you have a worry-free experience:

1. Travel Insurance:

- Prior to your trip, consider purchasing comprehensive travel insurance that covers medical emergencies, trip cancellations, and baggage loss. This can provide peace of mind in unforeseen situations.

2. Health Preparations:

- Before traveling to Canada, consult your healthcare provider regarding any recommended vaccinations or health precautions specific to your destination.

3. Medications and Prescriptions:

- Carry an ample supply of any prescribed medications you may need during your stay. Ensure you have proper documentation, including prescriptions, for these medications.

4. Stay Hydrated:

- Canada's climate can vary widely. In both cold and hot conditions, staying properly hydrated is essential. Carry a reusable water bottle to help you drink enough water throughout the day.

5. Traveler's Health Kit:

- Pack a basic traveler's health kit with items like pain relievers, bandages, antiseptic wipes, and any personal medications you may require.

6. Emergency Services:

- Familiarize yourself with the emergency phone number, which is 911 in Canada. This number can be dialed for police, fire, and medical emergencies.

7. Safety Precautions:

- While Canada is generally safe for travelers, it's wise to exercise common safety precautions. Keep an eye on your belongings, avoid displaying valuables in public, and be aware of your surroundings.

8. Weather Awareness:

- Check the weather forecast for your destination and pack accordingly. In colder months, dress warmly and in layers. In warmer months, protect yourself from the sun.

9. Wildlife Safety:

- If you plan to explore Canada's wilderness, educate yourself about local wildlife. Keep a safe distance from animals, carry bear spray in bear-prone areas, and follow park regulations.

10. Road Safety:

- If you're renting a car or driving in Canada, obey traffic laws, use seat belts, and be cautious in varying weather conditions, particularly during winter when roads may be icy.

11. Sun Protection:

- In sunny weather, wear sunscreen, sunglasses, and a wide-brimmed hat to protect yourself from harmful UV rays.

12. Food and Water:

- Canadian tap water is safe to drink in most areas, but if you have concerns, consider bottled water. Ensure that food is properly cooked and handled in restaurants.

13. Allergies and Dietary Needs:

- If you have food allergies or specific dietary requirements, communicate these clearly when dining out to ensure your safety.

14. Local Laws and Customs:

- Familiarize yourself with Canadian laws and customs, including regulations regarding cannabis use, which varies by province.

15. COVID-19 Precautions:

- Stay updated on any COVID-19 restrictions, requirements, and safety measures in place during your visit. Follow local guidelines and respect health protocols.

By following these safety and health tips, you can enjoy your visit to Canada with confidence, knowing that you've taken steps to protect your well-being and make the most of your experience in this beautiful country.

Handling Currency and Finances

When visiting Canada, it's essential to manage your finances and currency effectively. Here are some money-related tips to help you navigate financial matters during your trip:

1. Currency: Canada uses the Canadian Dollar (CAD) as its official currency. Familiarize yourself with the current exchange rate to understand the value of your currency in CAD.

2. Banking and ATMs:

- ATMs (Automatic Teller Machines) are widely available throughout Canada, especially in urban areas. They accept major international debit and credit cards. Check with your bank about any international fees that may apply.

3. Currency Exchange:

- Currency exchange services can be found at airports, banks, currency exchange offices, and some hotels. Compare rates to get the best deal, but be aware that exchange offices may charge commissions.

4. Credit and Debit Cards:

- Credit and debit cards, especially Visa and MasterCard, are widely accepted in Canada. Notify your bank of your travel plans to avoid card disruptions due to security measures.

5. Tipping:

- Tipping is customary in Canada, particularly in restaurants, bars, and for service providers like taxi drivers and tour guides. A typical tip is 15-20% of the bill before taxes.

6. Taxes:

- Canada has a Goods and Services Tax (GST) and a Provincial Sales Tax (PST) or Harmonized Sales Tax (HST), which vary by province. These taxes are usually included in the price of goods and services.

7. Budgeting:

- Plan your budget for accommodations, dining, transportation, and activities in advance. Canada can be an affordable or luxurious destination, depending on your choices.

8. Mobile Payments:

- Mobile payment apps like Apple Pay and Google Pay are widely accepted in Canada. Link your cards for convenient transactions.

9. Travel Insurance:

- Consider purchasing travel insurance that covers medical emergencies, trip cancellations, and lost baggage. It's essential for peace of mind during your trip.

10. Small Change:

- Keep some Canadian coins and small bills on hand for small purchases, transportation, and tipping.

11. Foreign Exchange Receipts:

- Keep receipts from currency exchange transactions as they may be required when converting Canadian currency back to your home currency.

12. Exchange Rate Apps:

- Download currency exchange rate apps to stay updated on real-time rates and make informed financial decisions.

13. Hidden Fees:

- Be aware of potential hidden fees, such as foreign transaction fees, when using credit cards. Check with your card issuer for details.

14. Security:

- Be cautious when using ATMs, and shield your PIN when entering it. Safeguard your cards and personal identification documents.

15. Currency Conversion:

- Some establishments may offer to convert your bill into your home currency at the point of sale. This may come with unfavorable exchange rates and additional fees, so it's often better to pay in CAD.

By keeping these money matters in mind, you can manage your finances efficiently and enjoy your trip to Canada without any financial hiccups.

Communication and Connectivity

In today's interconnected world, communication and staying connected while traveling are essential. Canada offers a range of options to keep you in touch with loved ones and stay informed during your visit:

1. Mobile Networks:

- Canada boasts an extensive mobile network coverage, with providers like Rogers, Bell, and Telus offering reliable service. Most urban and even many rural areas have good mobile reception.

2. SIM Cards:

- If you have an unlocked GSM-compatible phone, consider purchasing a local SIM card. You'll find SIM cards at convenience stores, airports, and mobile carrier shops. Prepaid plans offer various data and calling options.

3. International Roaming:

- Check with your mobile provider about international roaming options. While convenient, international roaming can be costly, so ensure you understand the rates and data limits.

4. Wi-Fi:

- Wi-Fi is widely available in Canada, with many hotels, cafes, restaurants, and public spaces offering free or paid Wi-Fi access. It's an excellent way to conserve data usage.

5. Internet Cafes:

- In urban areas, you may come across internet cafes where you can access the internet and make international calls at reasonable rates.

6. Mobile Apps:

- Download messaging apps like WhatsApp, Skype, or Facebook Messenger to stay in touch with friends and family via Wi-Fi or mobile data.

7. Emergency Services:

- The emergency phone number in Canada is 911, which you can dial for police, fire, and medical emergencies.

8. Postal Services:

- Canada Post provides postal services across the country. You can send mail, purchase stamps, and access other postal services at local post offices.

9. Language Considerations:

- While English is widely spoken and understood, Canada is bilingual, and French is the official language in some areas. In Quebec, you'll often find services and communication in French.

10. Travel Adapters:

- Canada uses Type A and Type B electrical outlets with a voltage of 120V and a frequency of 60Hz. Ensure you have the correct travel adapter for your devices.

11. Emergency Alerts:

- Canada has a national emergency alert system that sends alerts to mobile devices in the event of emergencies or severe weather conditions.

12. Satellite Phones:

- If you plan to explore remote areas without mobile coverage, consider renting or purchasing a satellite phone for emergency communication.

13. Public Payphones:

- Although becoming less common, public payphones are still available in Canada for making local and international calls.

14. Social Media:

- Stay updated with local news and events through social media platforms. Many businesses and attractions also have active social media profiles.

Staying connected in Canada is relatively straightforward, thanks to its well-developed communication infrastructure. Whether you prefer mobile data, Wi-Fi, or traditional phone services, you'll find various options to suit your needs and keep you connected while enjoying your Canadian adventure.

CONCLUSION

Embark on Your Canadian Adventure

Canada, with its breathtaking landscapes, rich cultural tapestry, and warm hospitality, awaits your exploration. From the rugged beauty of the Rocky Mountains to the charming streets of Old Quebec City, and from the stunning Niagara Falls to the vibrant cultural hubs of Toronto and Vancouver, this vast country offers a world of experiences.

As you plan your journey, remember the essential travel tips, safety precautions, and money matters outlined in this guide. Be open to discovering Canada's hidden gems, savoring its delectable cuisine, and immersing yourself in its diverse culture. Whether you're a nature enthusiast, an art lover, a foodie, or an adventure seeker, Canada has something extraordinary to offer you.

So, pack your bags, embrace the thrill of winter sports, savor the beauty of nature, and soak up the rich tapestry of history and culture. Canada welcomes you with open arms, ready to create memories that will last a lifetime.

Embark on your Canadian adventure, where every turn of the road and trail, every conversation with a local, and every encounter with its wonders will leave an indelible mark on your heart. The Great White North is calling, and its beauty and warmth are waiting to captivate your soul. Discover Canada and let your journey become an unforgettable chapter in your life's story.

Printed in Great Britain
by Amazon

29367315R00086